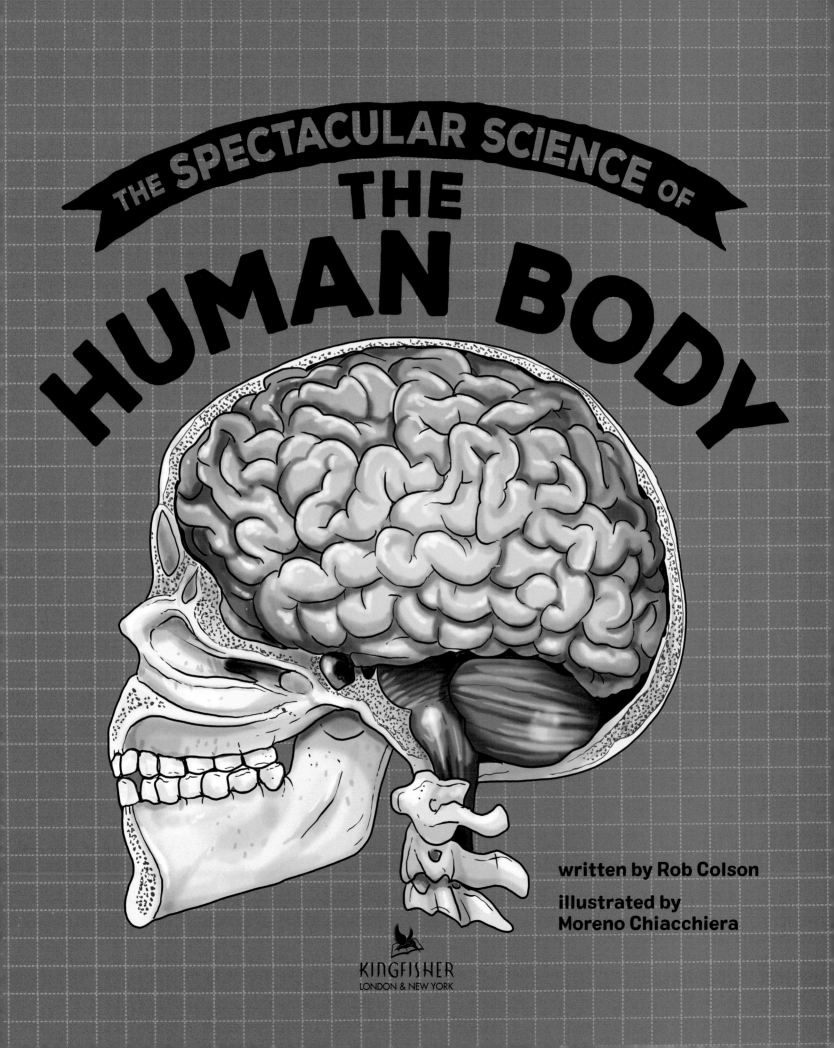

THE SPECTACULAR SCIENCE of
THE
HUMAN BODY

written by Rob Colson

illustrated by
Moreno Chiacchiera

KINGFISHER
LONDON & NEW YORK

KINGFISHER
LONDON & NEW YORK

First published 2023 by Kingfisher
an imprint of Macmillan Children's Books
The Smithson, 6 Briset Street,
London, EC1M 5NR
Associated companies
throughout the world
www.panmacmillan.com

EU representative: Macmillan Publishers
Ireland Limited, 1st Floor,
The Liffey Trust Centre, 117–126 Sheriff Street
Upper, Dublin 1, D01 YC43

Author: Rob Colson
Illustrator: Moreno Chiacchiera
Consultant: Nick Crumpton
Designed and edited by Tall Tree Ltd

ISBN: 978-0-7534-7916-2

Copyright © Macmillan Publishers
International Ltd 2023

A CIP record for this book is available
from the Library of Congress.

Printed in China
9 8 7 6 5 4 3 2 1
1TR/0823/WKT/RV/128MA

MIX
Paper | Supporting
responsible forestry
FSC® C116313
FSC
www.fsc.org

CONTENTS

A LIVING SYSTEM

Your body is a complex collection of different systems that work together to keep you alive.

CELLS

The smallest unit of the body is the cell (see pages 6–7). Cells can take a wide range of shapes and sizes, but most are so small that they cannot be seen by the naked eye.

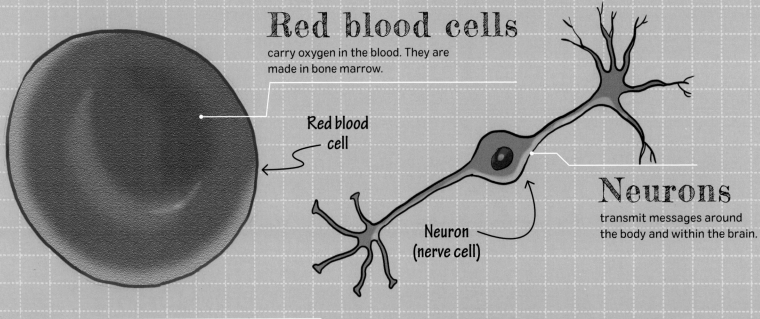

Osteocyte (bone cell)

Osteocytes

occupy small chambers within bones, surrounded by hard minerals.

Red blood cells

carry oxygen in the blood. They are made in bone marrow.

Red blood cell

Neuron (nerve cell)

Neurons

transmit messages around the body and within the brain.

TISSUES

Similar cells join together to form tissues. Connective tissue supports other tissue and binds them together. Connective tissues include bones, blood, tendons, and ligaments. Epithelial tissue provides a protective covering. Epithelial tissues include the skin and the linings of tubes in the body. Muscle tissue is made of cells that can contract and makes up muscles. Nervous tissue is made from neurons and transmits messages.

The four main types of tissue

Connective tissue

Epithelial tissue

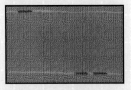

Muscle tissue

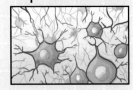

Nervous tissue

ORGANS

Tissues join together to form larger structures called organs. Organs carry out specific jobs in the body. For example, the heart pumps blood, while the stomach digests food. Organs work together in systems, and many organs take part in more than one system.

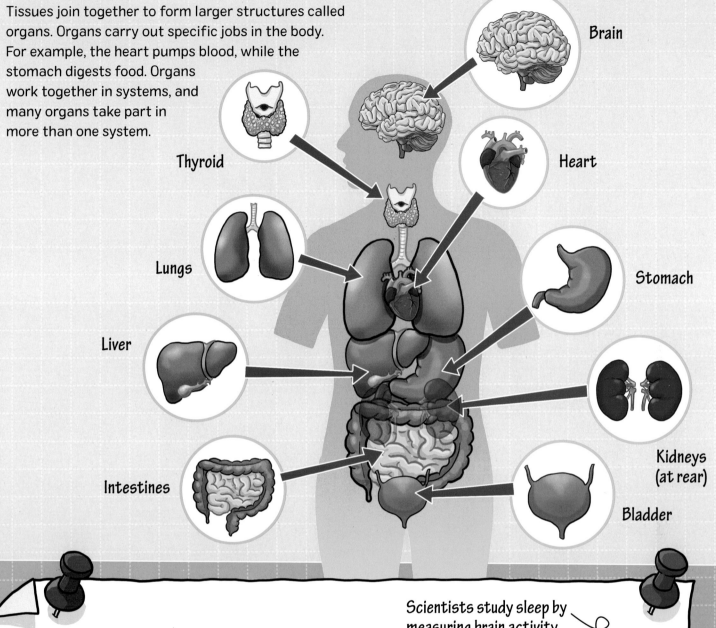

Brain

Thyroid

Heart

Lungs

Stomach

Liver

Kidneys (at rear)

Intestines

Bladder

BODY AND MIND

Conscious minds are produced by the action of the brain as it works with the rest of the body. Our minds create a picture of ourselves in the world, and this allows us to plan ahead and make decisions. Staying conscious requires a lot of effort. Every day, we need to turn off our conscious minds for several hours when we sleep.

Scientists study sleep by measuring brain activity.

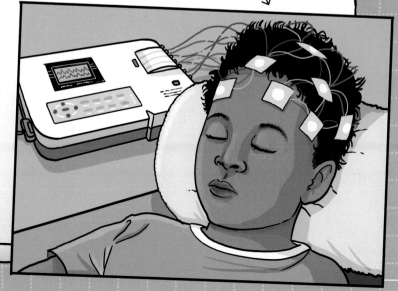

THE CELL

More than 1 million chemical reactions take place inside a cell every second!

Your body is made of more than 30 trillion cells. Cells contain smaller parts called organelles, each of which has a different job to do. Each tiny cell is a complex living system of its own.

Vacuoles store waste products.

STAYING BALANCED

Cells constantly monitor their internal state to keep the correct chemical balance. They take in just the right amount of nutrients from outside their cell wall to maintain a healthy mix of chemicals inside it. This process is called homeostasis.

Mitochondria

Most human cells contain mitochondria. These are the cells' energy packs. Mitochondria make a chemical called ATP (adenosine triphosphate). The ATP is sent around the cell to power all the different jobs it needs to do.

ANTONIE VAN LEEUWENHOEK

Dutch scientist Antonie van Leeuwenhoek (1632–1723) was one of the first people to study human cells using a microscope. He discovered sperm cells and gave an accurate description of the structure of red blood cells, which he described as "25,000 times smaller than a grain of sand."

Nucleus

At the center of most cells is the nucleus, which acts as the cell's control center. The nucleus is protected by a membrane. Tiny pores in the membrane allow molecules to pass in and out of the nucleus. The nucleus uses these molecules to communicate with the rest of the cell.

Centrioles help to organize the cell structure.

Ribosome

Ribosomes link together molecules called amino acids to make proteins, which are the body's main building blocks. The ribosomes can make about 20,000 different proteins.

Golgi body

The Golgi body packages up proteins to be transported from the cell.

Cell membrane

The cell membrane is a fatty layer that controls the movement of substances in and out of the cell. It protects the cell and ensures that its chemicals remain in a healthy balance.

THE SKELETON

The skeleton is a system of about 206 bones. The bones are connected by joints (see pages 10–11) to give the body strength and protection and allow it to move.

The axial skeleton (blue) forms the core of the body, protecting the vital organs.

The appendicular skeleton (yellow) forms the arms and legs.

Flat bones
Flat bones are thin bones with broad, flat surfaces. These bones, such as the skull bones and ribs, protect internal organs. Other flat bones such as the scapula (shoulder blade) act as points of attachment for muscles.

Irregular bones
Irregular bones, such as the vertebrae (back bones), have irregular, complicated shapes.

Clavicle

Scapula

Sternum

Humerus

Ribs

Vertebral column

Ulna

Radius

Ilium

STRUCTURE OF A BONE

Marrow
At the center of a bone, a hollow shaft contains yellow bone marrow, which stores fat. Red bone marrow in spongy bone makes red blood cells.

Compact bone gives the bone strength.

Periosteum
The periosteum is a thin outer membrane. It provides a blood supply to the bone.

Spongy bone is lightweight but strong.

Carpals

Metacarpals

Phalanges

Pubis

Ischium

Femur

Patella

Sesamoid bones
Sesamoid bones are not attached to other bones, but sit within tendons or muscles. The patella, or kneecap, is a sesamoid bone. Sitting in the quadriceps tendon, the patella acts as a pulley, providing a smooth surface for the tendon to slide over.

Fibula

Tibia

Tarsals

Metatarsals

Phalanges

Short bones
Short bones are cube-shaped bones that are found in the wrist and ankles. They allow flexible movements of the hands and feet.

Long bones
Long bones have a long, thin shape. They work like levers to give the body movement. The longest bone in the body is the femur, or thigh bone.

FLOATING BONE
The U-shaped hyoid is not attached to any other bone. It carries the weight of the tongue and allows you to swallow and to speak.

JOINTS

Bones meet at places called joints. Some joints allow lots of movement, while others hold the bones tightly in place.

Rigid joints
The lower jaw is the only movable bone in the skull. The other 21 bones are fused together at rigid joints that don't allow movement.

Hinge joints
Like a door hinge, these joints only allow movement back and forth in one plane. Examples include the elbow, knee, and finger joints.

Pivot joints
One bone rotates inside a ring created by a second bone. A pivot joint in your neck allows you to turn your head from side to side.

Ball-and-socket joints
The ball-shaped end of one bone sits inside the cup-shaped end of another. This allows movement in many different directions. Examples include the hips and shoulders.

Saddle joints
Two saddle-shaped ends of bones allow movement side to side and back and forth. The thumbs have saddle joints to allow lots of movement.

Gliding joints
Two bones have flat surfaces that glide over each other. These are found in the feet.

Ellipsoidal joints
The oval-shaped end of one bone sits inside an oval-shaped cup in a second bone. These are similar to ball-and-socket joints but have more restricted movement. They are found in the ankles and wrists.

MUSCLES

Muscles move bones at joints. They also make the heart beat and push food through the digestive system.

MUSCLE TISSUES

There are three kinds of muscle tissue. Skeletal muscles move the bones. Cardiac muscle pumps blood around the heart. Smooth muscle lines the walls of organs such as the stomach. Muscle tissue can contract (become shorter) or relax.

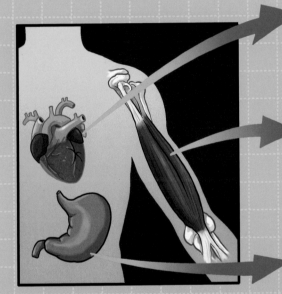

Cardiac muscle

Skeletal muscle

Smooth muscle

Sliding filaments

Muscles are made of bundles of long, cylindrical filaments. When a muscle relaxes, the thin filaments slide apart. When the muscle contracts, the thin filaments slide together.

Relaxed muscle

Thick filaments   Thin filaments

Contracted muscle

Thin filaments slide over thick filaments.

PAIR WORK

Muscles work in pairs to move the bones. The biceps and triceps muscles work together to bend or straighten the arm.

To straighten the arm, the triceps contracts and the biceps relaxes.

Triceps

Biceps

To bend the arm, the biceps contracts and the triceps relaxes.

LUIGI AND LUCIA GALVANI

In 1780, Italian doctor Luigi Galvani (1737–1798) and his wife Lucia (1743–1788) made the muscles in a dead frog's legs twitch by applying an electric spark to them. Their experiment mimicked the way nerve cells use electricity to stimulate muscle fibers.

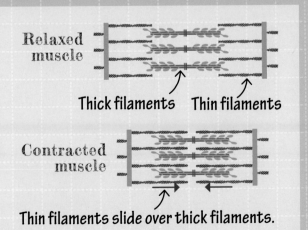

The dead frog's legs twitched when stimulated by electricity.

A PROTECTIVE BARRIER

The skin is the largest organ in the body. It helps us to control our temperature, prevents infection, and acts as a barrier against the outside world. It is made of three layers.

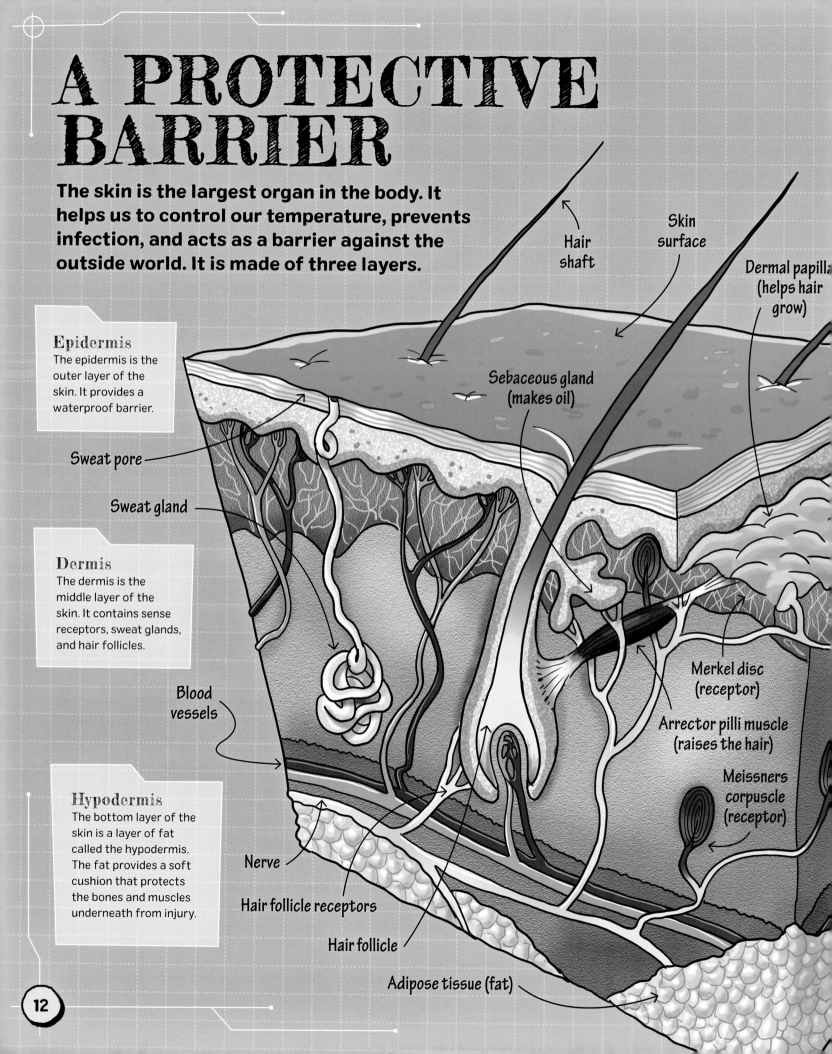

Hair shaft

Skin surface

Dermal papilla (helps hair grow)

Sebaceous gland (makes oil)

Epidermis
The epidermis is the outer layer of the skin. It provides a waterproof barrier.

Sweat pore

Sweat gland

Dermis
The dermis is the middle layer of the skin. It contains sense receptors, sweat glands, and hair follicles.

Blood vessels

Hypodermis
The bottom layer of the skin is a layer of fat called the hypodermis. The fat provides a soft cushion that protects the bones and muscles underneath from injury.

Merkel disc (receptor)

Arrector pilli muscle (raises the hair)

Meissners corpuscle (receptor)

Nerve

Hair follicle receptors

Hair follicle

Adipose tissue (fat)

TEMPERATURE CONTROL

For our bodies to function properly, we need to maintain an internal temperature of about 98.6°F.

When the body is in danger of overheating, blood is moved to the surface of the skin to lose heat. Sweat glands in the skin produce sweat, which evaporates from the surface of the skin. This evaporation also removes heat.

When the body is cold, blood vessels in the skin narrow. The skin becomes cold while the organs underneath stay warm. Goosebumps form when muscles at the base of hairs push them up straight. The erect hairs trap heat at the surface, although this works better for animals with thick fur!

Hair

Skin

Muscle relaxed

Goosebump

Muscle tensed

SUNBURN

The sun's rays contain invisible ultraviolet light, which can burn the skin. Sunburn damages the dermis. To protect against burning, the skin produces a pigment called melanin in the epidermis. The melanin blocks much of the ultraviolet light. However, some still gets through, and it is very dangerous even in small amounts, so it is important to protect the skin by applying suncream.

HAIR AND NAILS

Hair and nails contain a tough protein called keratin. Nails protect the tips of fingers and toes, while hair on your head keeps your head warm and protects it from sunburn. Hair and nails are made of dead cells, which is why it doesn't hurt when you cut them.

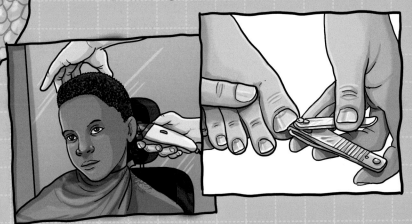

BODY BUGS

The skin is home to a range of micro-animals and microorganisms that are too small to see with the naked eye. Many of these organisms are harmless, but some cause diseases that need to be treated.

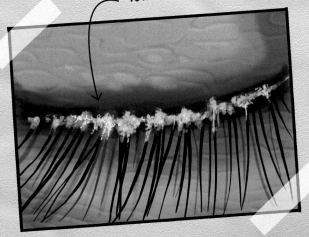

Eyelash mites gather in groups around the oily follicles of eyelashes.

EYELASH MITES

Eyelash mites (scientific name *Demodex*) are tiny creatures that live on hair follicles, feeding on hair cells and oils in the skin. The mites are related to spiders. They have eight legs, which they use to cling on to hairs. They measure just 0.012 inches long and are often found in bunches at the base of eyelashes. The mites are usually harmless and most people have eyelash mites living on them without even realizing it.

Abdomen

Legs have pincer-like claws.

BELLYBUTTON BACTERIA

The bellybutton is an ideal breeding ground for bacteria, fungi, and other microorganisms. More than 2,300 different kinds of bacteria have been found growing in people's bellybuttons, including the same bacteria that chefs use to make cheese!

ITCH MITES

Itch mites are similar in size to eyelash mites, but as their name suggests, itch mites are not harmless. They burrow under the outer layer of skin and feed on the blood. Eventually, this causes an itchy skin rash to develop. Itch mites can be cleared by thorough washing.

Female itch mites lay their eggs in a tunnel they burrow through the skin.

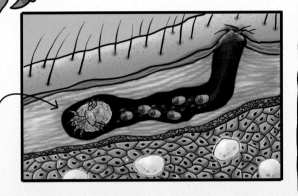

The mites burrow into a hair follicle with just their long abdomens sticking out.

Head

Pin-like mouthparts

ATHLETE'S FOOT

Athlete's foot is an itchy condition caused by a fungus that grows in the sweaty areas between people's toes.

Athlete's foot infects the top layer of skin.

THE CIRCULATORY SYSTEM

The circulatory system pumps blood around the body. The blood carries nutrients and oxygen to cells and takes away waste products. The system is powered by a constantly beating muscle—the heart.

FOUR CHAMBERS

The heart is divided into four chambers: two upper atria and two lower ventricles. The two chambers on the right-hand side receive blood from the body's cells and pump it to the lungs. The two chambers on the left-hand side receive blood from the lungs and pump it to the cells.

Your heart beats about

once per second

Each heartbeat follows the same cycle.

Superior vena cava (vein)

Aorta (artery)

Pulmonary artery (to lungs)

Pulmonary vein (from lungs)

Right atrium

Left atrium

Valves

Inferior vena cava (vein)

Right ventricle

Left ventricle

HOW A HEART BEATS

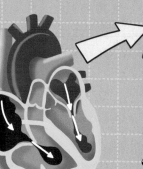

1 The walls of the atria and ventricles relax, allowing blood to flow into the heart from the veins.

2 The atria contract, squeezing blood into the ventricles.

3 The walls of the ventricles contract. This squeezes blood into the arteries. A valve between the ventricles and the atria closes at this point to stop blood from flowing back into the atria. The right ventricle pumps blood to the lungs, while the left ventricle pumps blood around the body.

CIRCULATION

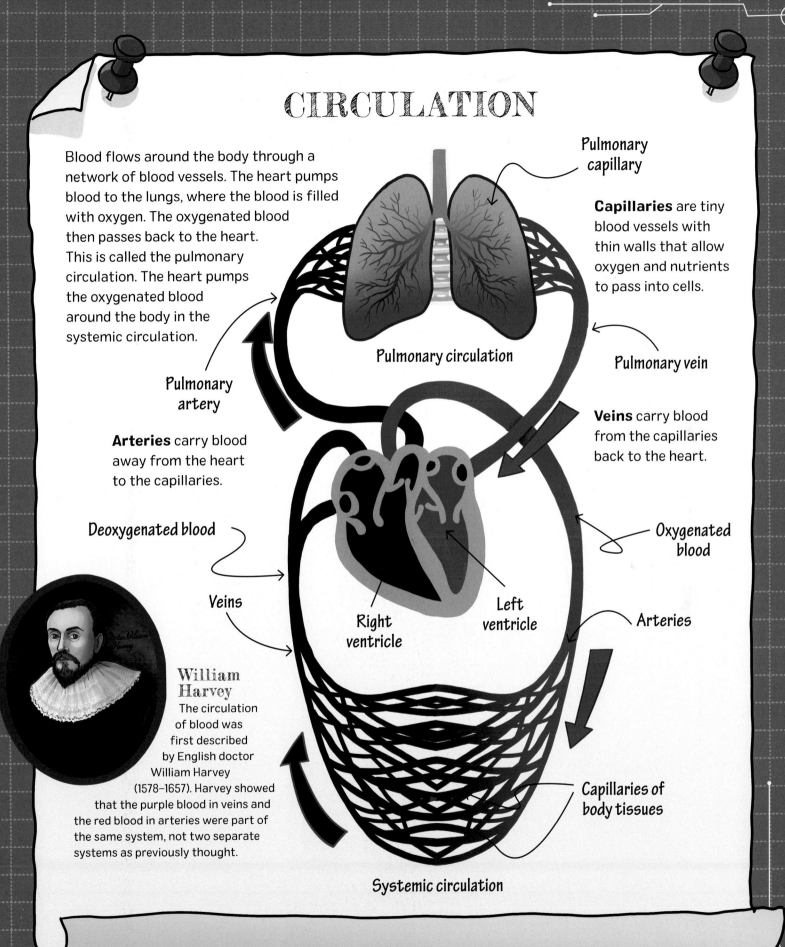

Blood flows around the body through a network of blood vessels. The heart pumps blood to the lungs, where the blood is filled with oxygen. The oxygenated blood then passes back to the heart. This is called the pulmonary circulation. The heart pumps the oxygenated blood around the body in the systemic circulation.

Pulmonary capillary

Capillaries are tiny blood vessels with thin walls that allow oxygen and nutrients to pass into cells.

Pulmonary circulation

Pulmonary vein

Pulmonary artery

Arteries carry blood away from the heart to the capillaries.

Veins carry blood from the capillaries back to the heart.

Deoxygenated blood

Oxygenated blood

Veins

Right ventricle

Left ventricle

Arteries

William Harvey

The circulation of blood was first described by English doctor William Harvey (1578–1657). Harvey showed that the purple blood in veins and the red blood in arteries were part of the same system, not two separate systems as previously thought.

Capillaries of body tissues

Systemic circulation

THE NERVOUS SYSTEM

The nervous system carries signals to and from the brain and spinal cord. It is made up of billions of neurons, or nerve cells.

Central
The central nervous system is made up of the brain and the spinal cord. This is the part of the nervous system that processes information and sends out signals.

Peripheral
The peripheral nervous system relays information between the central nervous system and the rest of the body.

The longest neurons
in the body are found in the sciatic nerve, which runs from the bottom of the spinal cord to the foot. In tall people, the sciatic nerve can be 3 feet long. It allows you to feel sensations in your feet and lower leg and controls the muscles that move them.

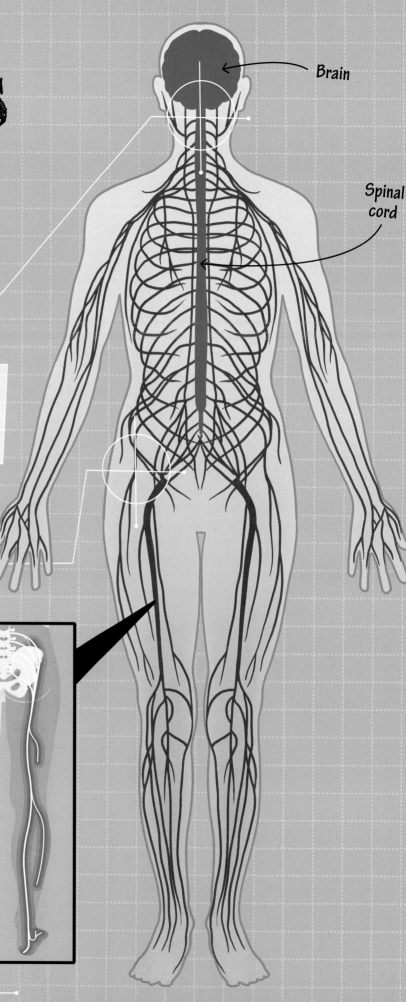

Brain

Spinal cord

NEURONS

Neurons both send and receive electrical signals. They send out their signal along a long, thin axon. They receive signals from other neurons through branching dendrites.

Dendrites

Nucleus

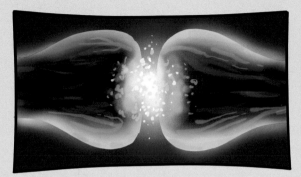

Synapse
The axon of one neuron meets the dendrite of another at a synapse. The neurons do not quite touch each other. Instead, the axon sends a signal to the dendrite by releasing chemicals across a tiny gap.

Myelin sheath
The myelin sheath is a fatty layer that insulates the axon, ensuring the electrical signal is sent quickly and efficiently.

← Axon

Reaction times
Neurons send signals at up to 400 feet per second. When athletes hear the gun at the start of a race, it takes their brains at least 80 milliseconds to hear the sound and send a signal to their muscles to move. This is known as the reaction time. If an athlete reacts more quickly than this, they have made a false start.

Direction of nerve impulse

Synapse

Axon terminals

REFLEXES

Some reactions don't involve the brain. Instead, the spinal cord sends a signal to muscles to react. The knee jerk reflex is caused by a tap on a spot below the knee cap. The spinal cord sends a signal to the thigh muscle to contract, kicking the foot up. This reaction takes just 50 milliseconds to happen.

Spinal cord

Receptor

Leg jerks up when knee is tapped.

Muscle

THE BRAIN

The brain contains about 85 billion neurons. Each neuron is connected to up to 10,000 other neurons, forming an ever-changing network of connections. Every second, your brain is constantly rewiring this network as it responds to the world.

PROTECTED ORGAN

The brain is about the size of a grapefruit. It is soft and squishy, a little like a blob of jelly, and it is easily damaged. For this reason, the brain is well protected inside the skull.

Cerebrum

The cerebrum is the largest part of the brain. It is covered by the cerebral cortex, which is a thin layer between 0.03 and 0.12 inches thick. The cortex is highly folded. This is the part of the brain that is responsible for processing information from the senses and problem-solving.

Cerebellum

The cerebellum (meaning "little brain") sits at the back of the head. It coordinates muscle movements and maintains balance.

Corpus callosum

Brainstem

The brainstem connects the cerebrum to the spinal cord and controls many of the body's unconscious functions, such as heart rate.

The cerebrum and cerebellum are divided into two hemispheres. The hemispheres of the cerebrum are connected by the corpus callosum, which allows them to communicate with one another.

CORTEX FUNCTIONS

Different parts of the cortex are involved in different jobs, such as processing information from the senses. Each of these sections is found on both hemispheres of the brain. One section may have several jobs.

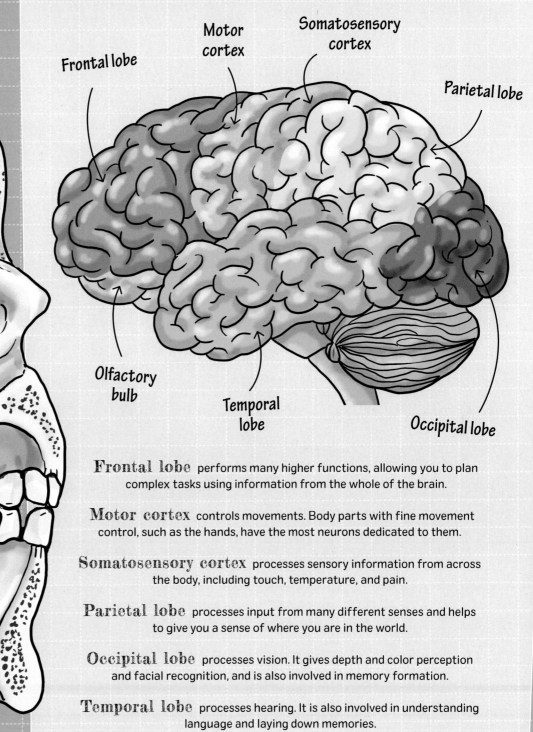

Frontal lobe

Motor cortex

Somatosensory cortex

Parietal lobe

Olfactory bulb

Temporal lobe

Occipital lobe

Frontal lobe performs many higher functions, allowing you to plan complex tasks using information from the whole of the brain.

Motor cortex controls movements. Body parts with fine movement control, such as the hands, have the most neurons dedicated to them.

Somatosensory cortex processes sensory information from across the body, including touch, temperature, and pain.

Parietal lobe processes input from many different senses and helps to give you a sense of where you are in the world.

Occipital lobe processes vision. It gives depth and color perception and facial recognition, and is also involved in memory formation.

Temporal lobe processes hearing. It is also involved in understanding language and laying down memories.

Olfactory bulb sits above the nose and processes the sense of smell.

VISION

Vision is one of the most important senses for humans. The information from our eyes allows our brains to form an image of the world around us.

BLIND SPOT

The point on the retina to which the optic nerve is connected cannot detect light. This causes a hole in the visual field called the blind spot. We do not normally notice our blind spots as our brains fill in the hole with a guess as to what is there.

Optic nerve

Blind spot

OPTIC NERVE

The optic nerve carries information to an area at the back of the brain called the visual cortex. Signals from the left eye are sent to the right visual cortex. Signals from the right eye are sent to the left visual cortex.

Retina

RETINA

The retina is a light-sensitive tissue at the back of the eye. Special sensors called photoreceptors turn the light into electrical signals, which are sent to the brain through the optic nerve. The image on the retina is upside-down. The brain turns the image the right way up again.

Fovea (sensitive central area of retina)

RODS AND CONES

The retina contains two kinds of photoreceptors. Rods see images in black-and-white and allow you to see in low light levels. Cones are responsible for color vision. There are three kinds of cone, each sensitive to different wavelengths of light: 60% of the cones sense the color red, which has the longest wavelength; 30% of the cones sense green; and 10% of the cones sense blue, which has the shortest wavelength.

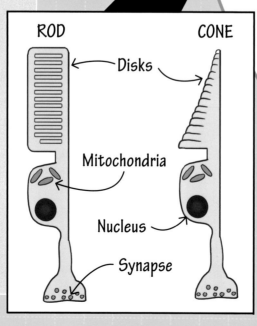

ROD

CONE

Disks

Mitochondria

Nucleus

Synapse

Retinal blood vessels

Conjunctiva (a protective clear membrane)

Sclera (white outer layer of the eyeball)

Vitreous body

IRIS
The iris is a muscle that changes size to make the pupil large in low light and small in bright light.

Iris

COLOR BLINDNESS
Some people lack one or more of kinds of cone. This makes them unable to sense certain colors. Red-green color blindness can occur when the green receptors don't work properly, making green look red. In this image, a person with full color vision will see the number 74. Someone who is red-green color blind sees the number 21. Some color blind people don't see any number at all!

Cornea

Pupil

Lens

LENS
As light passes through the lens, it focuses the image on the retina.

Ciliary body and muscle

BINOCULAR VISION
Each eye sees an object from a slightly different angle. The brain combines the two views to create a three-dimensional image of the world. This is known as binocular vision.

Vision through left eye

Vision through right eye

Combined view

HEARING

The ears sense vibrations in the air. We hear these vibrations as sounds.

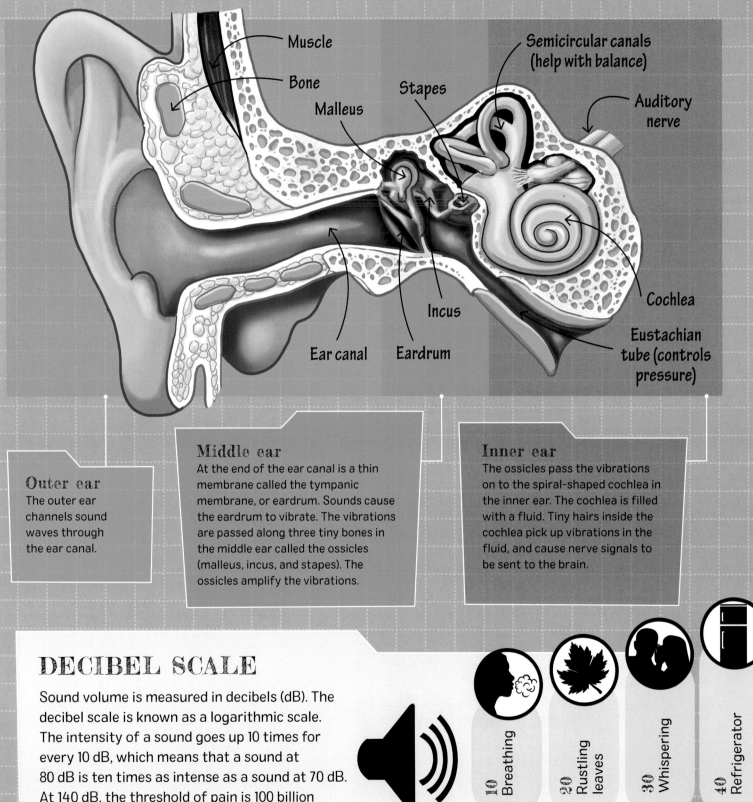

Muscle

Bone

Malleus

Stapes

Semicircular canals
(help with balance)

Auditory
nerve

Cochlea

Eustachian
tube (controls
pressure)

Incus

Ear canal

Eardrum

Outer ear
The outer ear
channels sound
waves through
the ear canal.

Middle ear
At the end of the ear canal is a thin
membrane called the tympanic
membrane, or eardrum. Sounds cause
the eardrum to vibrate. The vibrations
are passed along three tiny bones in
the middle ear called the ossicles
(malleus, incus, and stapes). The
ossicles amplify the vibrations.

Inner ear
The ossicles pass the vibrations
on to the spiral-shaped cochlea in
the inner ear. The cochlea is filled
with a fluid. Tiny hairs inside the
cochlea pick up vibrations in the
fluid, and cause nerve signals to
be sent to the brain.

DECIBEL SCALE

Sound volume is measured in decibels (dB). The
decibel scale is known as a logarithmic scale.
The intensity of a sound goes up 10 times for
every 10 dB, which means that a sound at
80 dB is ten times as intense as a sound at 70 dB.
At 140 dB, the threshold of pain is 100 billion
times as intense as the sound of whispering!

10 Breathing

20 Rustling
leaves

30 Whispering

40 Refrigerator

RANGE OF SOUNDS

Sound waves have an amplitude and a frequency. The amplitude is the loudness of the sound, while the frequency is its pitch—how high or low it sounds. Pitch is measured in hertz (Hz), which is the number of vibrations per second.

Amplitude

Wavelength (the shorter the wavelength, the higher the frequency)

We can detect sounds that range from 20 Hz to 20,000 Hz. Dogs can hear sounds as high as 50,000 Hz. A dog whistle makes a high-pitched sound that dogs can hear but humans cannot.

Distance to right ear

Sound source

Distance to left ear

SENSING DIRECTION

Sounds travel through air at a speed of 1,125 feet per second. The ears are spaced about 8 inches apart. This means that a sound coming from the right will reach the right ear about half a millisecond before it reaches the left ear. The sound will also be slightly louder in the right ear than the left. The brain detects small differences in timing and loudness to work out the direction the sound is coming from.

50 Moderate rainfall

60 Conversation

70 Vacuum cleaner

80 Truck

90 Hairdryer

100 Helicopter

110 Trombone

120 Police siren

130 Jet engine

140 Fireworks

Sounds above 85 decibels can be harmful

OTHER SENSES

We often think of five main senses: seeing, hearing, touching, tasting, and smelling. However, there are many other senses, including a sense of temperature and a sense of body position.

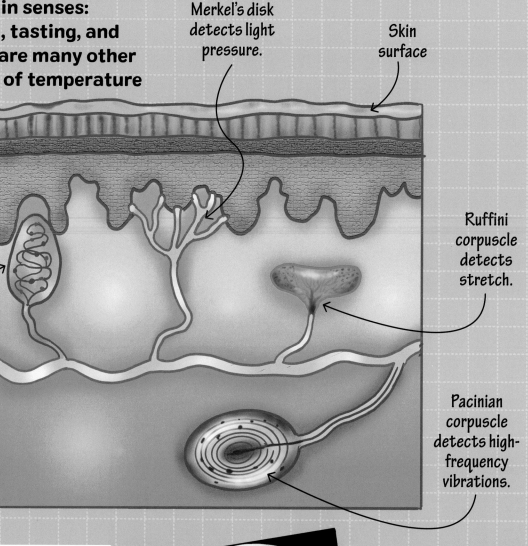

Merkel's disk detects light pressure.

Skin surface

Meissner's corpuscle detects pressure and low frequency vibrations.

Ruffini corpuscle detects stretch.

Pacinian corpuscle detects high-frequency vibrations.

TOUCH

There are three main kinds of touch receptor in the dermis layer of the skin. Mechanoreceptors sense pressure. Thermoreceptors sense temperature. Pain receptors send out pain signals if the skin is damaged. Pain receptors are found throughout the body.

SENSITIVE FINGERS

The fingertips are packed full of mechanoreceptors. They are also covered in swirls of raised lines, which create your fingerprint. Fingerprints greatly increase the sensitivity of fingers. The ridges of fingerprints magnify the size of tiny vibrations when we run our fingers across a surface, allowing the Pacinian corpuscles to detect them.

Fingertip

Fingerprint

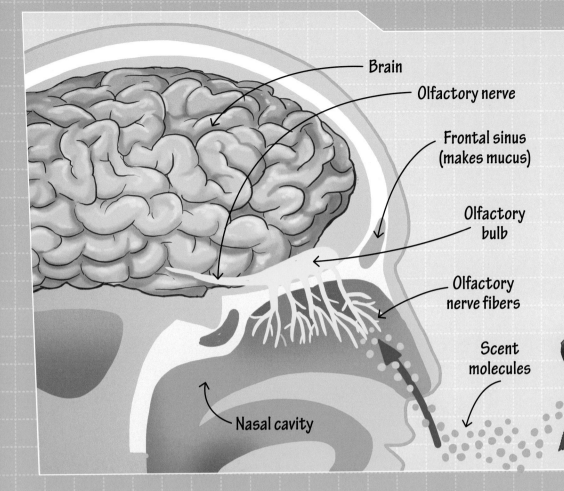

Brain

Olfactory nerve

Frontal sinus (makes mucus)

Olfactory bulb

Olfactory nerve fibers

Scent molecules

Nasal cavity

SMELL

Our noses detect tiny amounts of chemicals in the air. Scent particles dissolve in the mucus lining of the nose and are detected by sensors, which send a signal to the brain via the olfactory bulb. The sensors can detect 10,000 different odors.

TASTE

We taste our food using sensors in our mouths called taste buds, which are contained in bumps called papillae. We can detect five kinds of flavor: sweet, sour, salty, bitter, and umami (savory). The full sensation of the flavor of food comes from a combination of its taste and its smell.

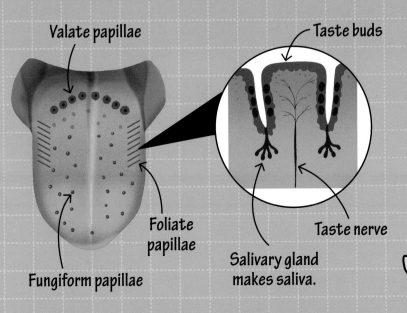

Valate papillae

Taste buds

Foliate papillae

Taste nerve

Salivary gland makes saliva.

Fungiform papillae

SENSING THE SELF

In addition to sensing the outside world, the body also senses itself. Sensors inside muscles send messages to the brain and spinal cord to say what position each part of the body is in and how it is moving. This is a sense called proprioception.

Standing on one leg with your eyes closed, you rely on proprioception to make small adjustments and stay balanced.

THE DIGESTIVE SYSTEM

When you eat, your food starts on a long journey through your body. It takes up to three days for some kinds of food to pass right through the digestive system.

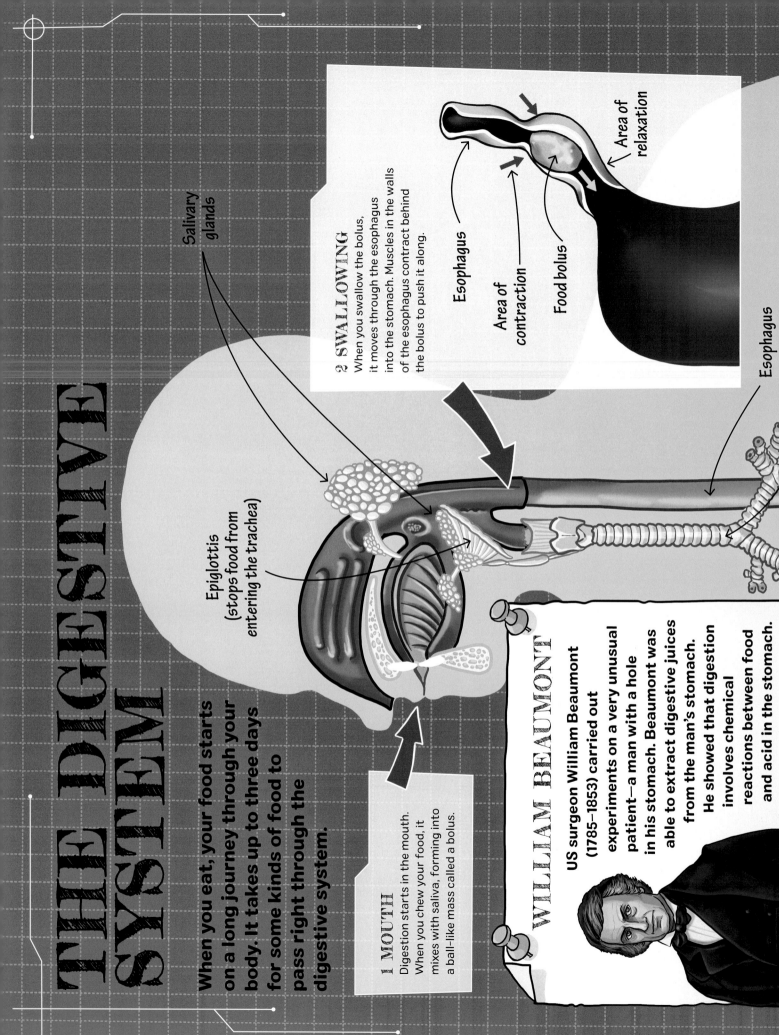

Salivary glands

Epiglottis (stops food from entering the trachea)

2 SWALLOWING

When you swallow the bolus, it moves through the esophagus into the stomach. Muscles in the walls of the esophagus contract behind the bolus to push it along.

Esophagus

Area of contraction

Food bolus

Area of relaxation

Esophagus

Trachea (windpipe)

1 MOUTH

Digestion starts in the mouth. When you chew your food, it mixes with saliva, forming into a ball-like mass called a bolus.

WILLIAM BEAUMONT

US surgeon William Beaumont (1785–1853) carried out experiments on a very unusual patient—a man with a hole in his stomach. Beaumont was able to extract digestive juices from the man's stomach. He showed that digestion involves chemical reactions between food and acid in the stomach.

3 STOMACH

Food stays in the stomach for between four and six hours. Digestive juices break the food up into smaller pieces to form a liquid called chyme. The digestive juices contain hydrochloric acid, which kills nearly all the bacteria that may be in the food, protecting the body against food poisoning.

5 LARGE INTESTINE

From the small intestine, the remains of the food pass into the large intestine. The large intestine absorbs water from the remains, leaving the waste product feces.

6 ANUS

Feces remains in the large intestine for up to 48 hours before it passes out of the body through the anus.

Gall bladder   Liver

Pancreas

4 SMALL INTESTINE

The chyme passes from the stomach into the small intestine – a narrow curled-up tube about 16 feet long. As the chyme passes along the small intestine, nutrients are absorbed into the blood through thousands of finger-like villi. The villi increase the surface area of the small intestine to over 300 square feet.

Villi

Single villus

Epithelial cells

Nerves

Lymphatic vessel

Capillaries

Vein

Artery

29

FILTERING THE BLOOD

Many substances that enter the blood are potentially damaging to the body. The kidneys and liver both filter blood to make sure these substances are removed.

Nephrons make urine as they filter the blood. Each kidney contains about 1 million nephrons.

KIDNEYS

The kidneys remove excess water, salts, and harmful waste from the blood, making urine. Inside the kidneys, the blood passes through tiny filters called nephrons. The filtered blood leaves the kidneys to travel back to the heart, while the urine is passed from the kidneys to the bladder through the ureters.

Renal artery

Glomorulus (network of capillaries)

Bowman's capsule (filter)

Kidney

Ureter

Bladder

The body makes

1-2 quarts

of urine per day.

BLADDER

The bladder is a stretchy bag that can hold more than 25 ounces of urine. When it is about half-full, stretch sensors on the bladder send a signal to the brain that it is time to go to the toilet and empty the bladder.

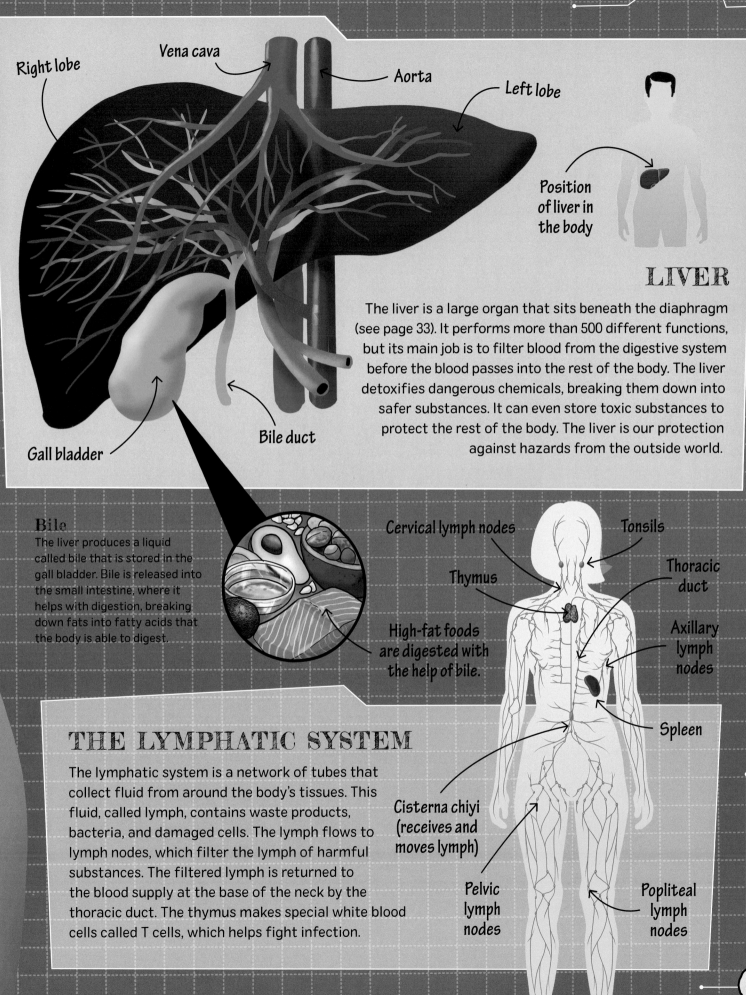

Right lobe

Vena cava

Aorta

Left lobe

Position of liver in the body

LIVER

The liver is a large organ that sits beneath the diaphragm (see page 33). It performs more than 500 different functions, but its main job is to filter blood from the digestive system before the blood passes into the rest of the body. The liver detoxifies dangerous chemicals, breaking them down into safer substances. It can even store toxic substances to protect the rest of the body. The liver is our protection against hazards from the outside world.

Bile duct

Gall bladder

Bile

The liver produces a liquid called bile that is stored in the gall bladder. Bile is released into the small intestine, where it helps with digestion, breaking down fats into fatty acids that the body is able to digest.

High-fat foods are digested with the help of bile.

Cervical lymph nodes

Tonsils

Thymus

Thoracic duct

Axillary lymph nodes

Spleen

THE LYMPHATIC SYSTEM

The lymphatic system is a network of tubes that collect fluid from around the body's tissues. This fluid, called lymph, contains waste products, bacteria, and damaged cells. The lymph flows to lymph nodes, which filter the lymph of harmful substances. The filtered lymph is returned to the blood supply at the base of the neck by the thoracic duct. The thymus makes special white blood cells called T cells, which helps fight infection.

Cisterna chiyi (receives and moves lymph)

Pelvic lymph nodes

Popliteal lymph nodes

THE RESPIRATORY SYSTEM

The respiratory system is responsible for breathing. We breathe in oxygen from the air and breathe out carbon dioxide. We need to keep breathing as it enables vital chemical reactions inside cells.

THE LUNGS

The lungs are two large sacs in your chest. They are filled with hundreds of millions of tiny air sacs called alveoli. The alveoli have very thin walls, which allow oxygen to pass from the air into the blood, and carbon dioxide to pass from the blood into the air.

Pulmonary vein carries oxygenated blood.

Alveoli are located at the ends of the bronchioles.

Pulmonary artery carries deoxygenated blood.

Nose

Mouth

Trachea

Bronchus

Bronchioles

Lung

BREATHING

When you breathe in, a muscle underneath the lungs called the diaphragm contracts, pulling it flat, while muscles between the ribs contract to pull the rib cage up. This creates more space within the body for the lungs to expand, sucking air in through trachea from the nose and mouth. When you breathe out, the diaphragm and rib muscles relax. This presses on the lungs, pushing air out through the trachea.

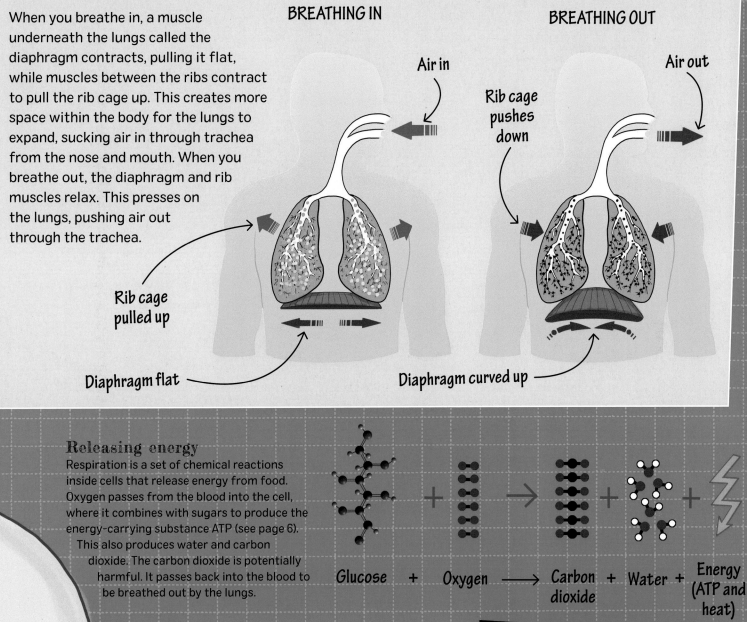

BREATHING IN

Air in

Rib cage pulled up

Diaphragm flat

BREATHING OUT

Air out

Rib cage pushes down

Diaphragm curved up

Releasing energy

Respiration is a set of chemical reactions inside cells that release energy from food. Oxygen passes from the blood into the cell, where it combines with sugars to produce the energy-carrying substance ATP (see page 6). This also produces water and carbon dioxide. The carbon dioxide is potentially harmful. It passes back into the blood to be breathed out by the lungs.

Glucose + Oxygen ⟶ Carbon dioxide + Water + Energy (ATP and heat)

HANS KREBS

British-German biochemist Hans Krebs (1900–1981) discovered the series of chemical reactions that release energy from food during respiration. This is now known as the Krebs cycle. These reactions can also happen in the reverse direction, for instance when plants use the energy of the Sun to make sugars.

THE ENDOCRINE SYSTEM

The endocrine system is made up of a network of glands that produce chemical messengers called hormones. The hormones are released into the bloodstream and reach every cell in the body, producing a wide variety of effects.

Hypothalamus

Pituitary gland

Pineal gland

Brain
There are three glands inside the brain. The hypothalamus and pituitary gland produce a range of hormones that control the production of hormones by other glands. The pineal gland produces hormones that control sleep patterns.

Thyroid
The thyroid gland produces hormones that control the speed at which your cells work.

Thymus
The thymus stimulates the production of T cells, a type of white blood cell that fights disease.

Adrenal glands
These sit above the kidneys. They produce hormones called adrenaline and noradrenaline, which prepare the body for action in dangerous situations.

Pancreas
This organ produces insulin, a hormone that regulates blood sugar levels.

Gonads (testes in males and ovaries in females)
These glands produce sex hormones. The testes produce testosterone, which stimulates sperm production and affects body and bone mass. The ovaries produce estrogen and progesterone, which regulate a woman's reproductive cycle (see page 43). They also produce small amounts of testosterone.

Testes (male)

Ovaries (female)

SLOW AND FAST

Some hormones act on the body very slowly. The growth hormone produced by the pituitary gland causes the body to grow throughout childhood. Growth hormone levels are highest during puberty, when bodies experience a rapid growth spurt.

American Robert Wadlow (1918–1940) had an enlarged pituitary gland that produced too much growth hormone. Wadlow was already as tall as an adult man aged seven, and he was still growing when he died aged 22. Standing 8 feet, 11 inches tall, he was the tallest person ever recorded.

Robert Wadlow standing next to his father.

Dorothy Hodgkin

British chemist Dorothy Crowfoot Hodgkin (1910–1994) worked out the three-dimensional structure of many important molecules in the body, including the hormone insulin. Her discovery enabled the mass-production of insulin for the treatment of diabetes.

Some hormones act very quickly. Adrenaline produces a range of changes in the body within just a few seconds. These changes prepare the body for immediate action.

1 Pupils of the eye widen
2 Heart rate increases
3 Skin sweats
4 Blood is sent to muscles
5 Hairs stand on end
6 Digestion slows, causing butterflies in the stomach
7 Breathing increases
8 Blood pressure goes up

HEALING THE BODY

When you are injured or get sick, your body has a number of ways to make you better.

WHITE BLOOD CELLS

White blood cells have the job of protecting the body from infectious diseases. White blood cells called phagocytes identify and destroy pathogens, which are harmful viruses, bacteria, or other microorganisms. White blood cells "eat" pathogens in a process called phagocytosis.

A white blood cell can attack many pathogens at once by extending out thin arms called pseudopodia.

BLOOD CLOTS

When the wall of a blood vessel is broken, platelets in the blood are called into action. They change shape from round to spiny and stick to each other across the gap. The platelets combine with proteins in the blood to form a substance called fibrin. Strands of fibrin form a net, which traps more platelets and red blood cells to plug the gap. This blood clot protects the tissues underneath while they repair themselves.

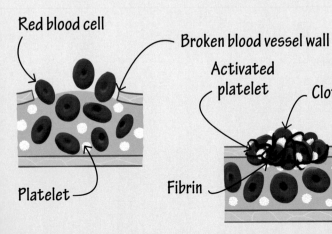

Red blood cell

Broken blood vessel wall

Activated platelet

Clot

Platelet

Fibrin

LOUIS PASTEUR

French chemist Louis Pasteur (1822–1895) developed the germ theory of disease. He showed that diseases can be spread by invisible microbes in the air. Inspired by Pasteur's work, surgeons started to sterilize wounds during surgery to stop them from becoming infected.

FIRST LINE OF DEFENSE

The best way to stay healthy is to avoid taking in harmful substances in the first place. The skin forms a barrier to most invaders. Tears keep the eyes moist and also attack and kill germs. Mucus in your nose traps particles in the air so that they can be swallowed and dealt with by the strong acid in the stomach. Sneezing also clears the nose of unwanted irritants. Washing your hands can help to stop germs spreading.

REPAIRING BONES

When a bone fractures, or breaks, it can heal itself. A cast will stop the bone from moving whilst it heals. There are three stages to the healing process.

1 A blood clot, or hematoma, forms around the fracture.

2 After a few days, a type of soft bone called callus replaces the blood clot. The callus gradually hardens over the next few weeks.

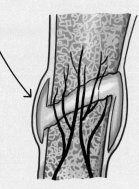

3 Over the following months, regular bone replaces the hard callus in a process called remodeling.

REPRODUCTION

Reproduction starts when a man's sperm fertilizes a woman's egg inside the woman's fallopian tube. This creates a single-celled zygote. The zygote starts to divide to form a small bundle of cells called a blastocyst.

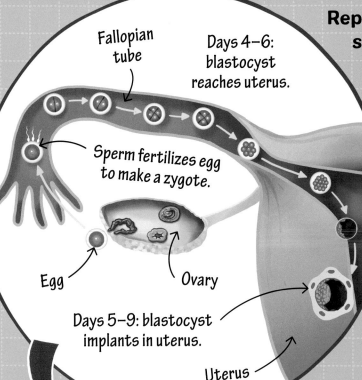

Fallopian tube

Days 4–6: blastocyst reaches uterus.

Sperm fertilizes egg to make a zygote.

Egg

Ovary

Days 5–9: blastocyst implants in uterus.

Uterus

Toward the womb

In the first week after fertilization, the blastocyst moves down the fallopian tube to the uterus, or womb. It burrows into the soft lining of the uterus. At this stage, it is only 0.008 inches in diameter. Safely embedded in the uterus, the dividing cells start to become different from one another and an embryo develops.

8 weeks

The arms and legs have started growing, and it is recognizably a human shape. It is now called a fetus.

THE DEVELOPING FETUS

The embryo develops rapidly in the uterus, taking nutrients from the mother's blood. After a few weeks, it starts to take human shape and is known as a fetus.

4 weeks

The embryo's internal organs have started to develop. It is about the size of a pea.

Placenta provides oxygen and nutrients.

Uterus

Amniotic sac provides protection.

Umbilical cord

Embryo

Fetus has turned around ready for birth.

16 weeks
The fetus can blink its eyes and suck its thumb. It is now about 5 inches long.

32 weeks
The lungs are fully developed and the brain is developing rapidly. The fetus has grown to 16 inches long.

VIRGINIA APGAR

US doctor Virginia Apgar (1909–1974) developed a set of tests to measure a newborn baby's health. Applied immediately after birth, the tests have greatly reduced the rate of infant deaths by identifying problems the baby may be having with its breathing, circulation, or other vital systems.

Birth
The baby is born around 40 weeks after the egg was fertilized.

Belly button
Inside the uterus, the foetus is connected to the placenta by the umbilical cord. It receives oxygen and nutrients from the mother's blood via the placenta. When the baby is born, the umbilical cord is cut, leaving behind a belly button.

THE CODE FOR LIFE

With the exception of red blood, hair, and nail cells, each of our cells contains the complete instructions for how to make a body. These instructions take the form of 23 pairs of chromosomes inside the cell nucleus.

James Watson   Francis Crick

Discovering the double-helix

The double-helix structure of DNA was discovered in 1953 by James Watson (born 1928) and Francis Crick (1916–2004), using X-ray images produced by their colleagues Rosalind Franklin, Raymond Gosling, and Maurice Wilkins. The discovery helped to solve the mystery of how DNA codes for life.

DNA

A chromosome is made of a single molecule of deoxyribonucleic acid (DNA). The DNA molecule is a double-helix with two strands that wind around one another. The strands are connected to one another by a series of up to 300 million base pairs.

Sense strand

Guanine (G) pairs with cytosine

Cytosine (C) pairs with guanine

Thymine (T) pairs with adenine

Adenine (A) pairs with thymine

Antisense strand

BASE PAIRS

Bases are formed from four different chemicals: guanine (G), cytosine (C), thymine (T), and adenine (A). Guanine on one strand always pairs with cytosine on the other strand, while thymine always pairs with adenine. Each base pair takes one of four values, read along the sense strand: G, C, T, or A.

CODONS

Groups of three base pairs are called codons. Each codon can take one of 64 different values. The codons code for chemicals called amino acids, plus the instructions START and STOP. For example, the codon GAG codes for the amino acid glutamate. Amino acids join together to form larger molecules called proteins, which are the building blocks of our bodies. Protein molecules are made of chains of up to 2,000 amino acids.

Sense strand

C C C

T C A

G A G

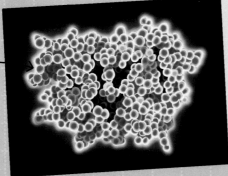

Protein molecule

GENES

The main job of DNA is to code for the creation of proteins. The thousands of proteins in the human body are all made using combinations of the same 20 amino acids. Groups of codons code for specific proteins. These groups of codons are called genes.

GENETIC INHERITANCE

A human cell contains about 25,000 genes. We inherit roughly half of our genes from each of our parents. This means that we share 50 per cent of our genes with our parents and our siblings. These are our closest relatives, and we are likely to look a lot like them. Identical twins grow from the same fertilized egg. They share 100 percent of their genes with one another.

A COMMON ANCESTOR

All living things contain DNA, and the DNA of all life on Earth codes for amino acids in exactly the same way. This is because we share a common ancestor from billions of years ago. Every living thing on Earth is related to every other living thing!

GROWING UP

It takes many years for a human to grow from a baby to an adult. Throughout this period, the body undergoes huge changes and the brain learns countless new skills.

BABIES

A newborn baby is completely dependent on its parents. However, the baby is learning all the time. In the first few months, the baby will learn to focus its eyes and start exploring the world around it.

INFANCY AND CHILDHOOD

Over the first couple of years of life, an infant learns how to walk and how to speak. In early childhood, they will learn complex physical skills such as riding a bike and mental skills such as reading.

PUBERTY

Puberty is a period of rapid change as a child's body takes on an adult shape.

Girls

In girls, puberty commonly starts around age 10-11. The girl's breasts start to grow and she undergoes a growth spurt. The hips widen and hair grows in the pubic area. About 2 years after the start of puberty, a girl's periods start. These are part of the menstrual cycle, a monthly series of changes in an adult woman's body.

Boys

Puberty normally starts about a year later for boys than girls. The boy's penis and testes grow larger and he undergoes a growth spurt. The chest and shoulders become broader, and hair grows in the pubic area. About 2 years after the start of puberty, a boy's voice breaks. This happens because the voice box, or larynx, becomes larger.

CLUMSY TEENS

During puberty, the brain struggles to keep up with the rapid changes that are happening in the body. During a growth spurt, the brain has to relearn how to control a different, bigger body, and for a while a teenager may become clumsy. The clumsiness goes away once the growth spurt has ended.

DEVELOPING BRAIN

Our brains continue to develop until our mid-20s, but the first year of life sees the most rapid changes. The brain of a newborn baby rapidly makes new synapses, and the brain of a one-year-old has twice as many connections as an adult brain. This is a period of rapid learning. Many of these connections disappear through childhood in a process called synaptic pruning. Only the pathways through the brain that prove useful are kept.

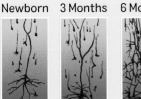

Newborn 3 Months 6 Months 2 Years 4 Years 6 Years

Synapse formation   Synaptic pruning

BIONIC BODIES

When our bodies stop working properly or when we lose a body part, we quickly realize how easily bodies can go wrong. In recent years, scientists have made amazing advances in producing replacement body parts.

Opposable thumb

Nerves attached at shoulder

Hinged elbow joint

BIONIC LIMBS

Bionic limbs are artificial arms or legs that are linked up to nerves in the body so that the brain can control them. Instructions from the brain are sent along the nerves to a computer in the limb, which converts them into instructions for the limb's artificial muscles. In 2014, American Les Baugh, a man who had lost both his arms, was able to perform a variety of tasks using bionic arms. After a period of training, Les could control the arms with his thoughts.

Simple movements are complicated!

Many things are going on in your body when you perform a simple action such as scratching your nose. You need to raise your arm, bend your elbow, rotate your forearm, and extend your finger to just the right place. You then need to move the finger with the right amount of pressure to stop the itch. This process involves continuous communication between your arm and your brain, all done in a fraction of a second.

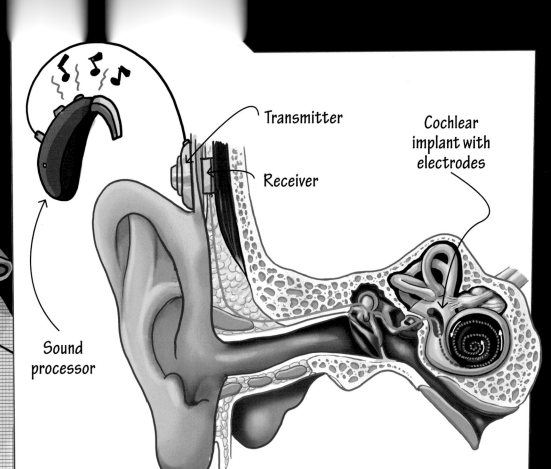

Transmitter

Cochlear implant with electrodes

Receiver

Sound processor

BIONIC EARS

Cochlear implants are hearing aids that can give a sense of hearing to someone who is completely deaf. A microphone placed near the ear picks up sounds and radios them to a receiver implanted in the cochlea. The receiver converts the sounds into electrical signals that are passed directly to the auditory nerve, which sends them to the brain.

Bionic touch

Communication between brain and limb works both ways. The brain tells the limb how to move, but the limb also sends back crucial information such as the sense of touch. This is how you know how hard to scratch an itch. The next generation of bionic limbs will have pressure sensors fitted to them. These sensors will be connected to the sensory cortex, the part of the brain that processes the senses.

BIONIC HEARTS

Patients with failing hearts may be fitted with a total artificial heart (TAH) while they await a heart transplant. The TAH replaces the heart's two lower chambers, the ventricles, which pump blood through the body. It is connected to an electric driver, which can be carried around in a bag.

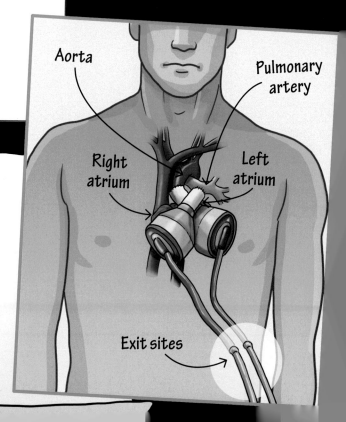

Aorta

Pulmonary artery

Right atrium

Left atrium

Exit sites

GLOSSARY

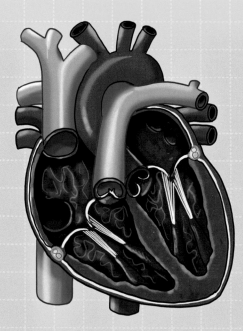

Artery
A blood vessel that carries blood away from the heart.

Atria
(singular atrium) The two top chambers of the heart into which blood enters from the veins.

Bacteria
Simple single-celled organisms. Our bodies are home to trillions of bacteria. Some make us ill, while others help to perform important jobs such as digestion.

Capillaries
Tiny blood vessels with thin walls that allow oxygen and nutrients to pass into cells from the blood and waste products to pass into the blood from the cells.

Cell
The smallest working unit of a body. A human body is made of about 30 trillion cells.

Chromosome
A long molecule of DNA (deoxyribonucleic acid) that contains genetic information. A cell nucleus contains 46 chromosomes.

Fungus
A group of organisms that includes yeast, mold, and mushrooms. Various kinds of fungus can infect human bodies.

Gene
A section of a chromosome that contains a particular set of information, such as the instructions to make a protein.

Homeostasis
The maintenance of a healthy internal balance within a body, an organ, or an individual cell.

Hormone
A chemical that is released into the blood to control the actions of cells or organs.

Joint
A place at which two bones meet. Some joints fix bones in place, while others allow certain kinds of movement.

Mitochondria
(singular mitochondrion) Structures inside cells that release energy.

Muscle
A body tissue that can contract. Muscles work together to move body parts.

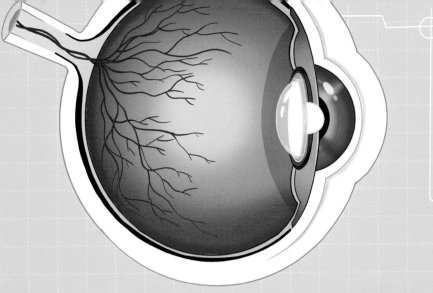

Neuron
Also called a nerve cell, a type of cell that sends and receives electrical messages.

Nucleus
A structure with a membrane inside cells that contains the cell's chromosomes.

Organ
A part of the body made of a number of tissues that work together to perform a particular job or set of jobs.

Photoreceptors
Cells in the eye that sense light. Rods sense color, while cones allow us to see in black-and-white in low light.

Platelets
Small fragments of cells in the blood that help the blood to clot.

Proprioception
A sense that allows us to keep track of the positions of different parts of our bodies.

Synapse
A tiny gap across which two neurons communicate with each other.

Tendon
A strong, flexible cord that connects muscles to bones.

Tissue
A group of similar cells that perform a particular job in the body.

Trachea
Also called the windpipe, a tube that carries air between the lungs and the mouth.

Uterus
Also called the womb, the organ in a woman's body inside which a fetus grows and develops.

Vein
A blood vessel that carries blood toward the heart.

Ventricles
The two lower chambers of the heart, which forcefully pump blood into the arteries.

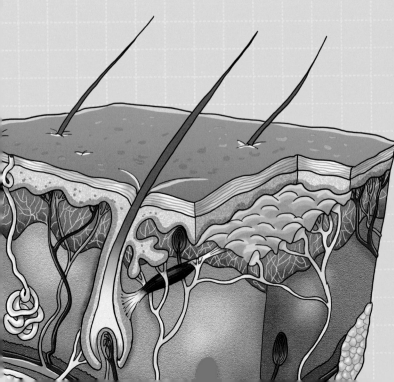

INDEX